THE ENTREPRENEURS HANDBOOK

THE ENTREPRENEURS HANDBOOK

10 Steps to Launching a Startup

HARPER NORTHWOOD

QuantumQuill Press

CONTENTS

CHAPTER 1

Introduction

Move over Fortune 500 companies, now is the time for innovative business ideas led by visionaries and innovators who will not yield to fears and small thinking. According to the Kauffman Index of Entrepreneurial Activity (KIEA), in the U.S. alone, in 2009, 558,000 new businesses were founded per month, with 27 percent of KIEA entrepreneurs coming from the businesses closing metric. Despite economic downturns, business startups are still as vital as in the years before. They are the ultimate test because the bar for innovating a business model cannot be set any higher than during difficult economic times. If you are considering a career in entrepreneurship, this guide will help you prepare and climate the storm, ultimately resulting in great rewards should you possess the necessary skills and determination to succeed.

Welcome to The Entrepreneur's Handbook: 10 Steps to Launching a Startup. This online handbook provides the essential information you need through every stage of the entrepreneurial process, from mapping out initial plans and funding your company to growing your business and putting together a team. Attaining just the right mix of hard work and risk is vital to the delicate balance of your entrepreneurial spirit, while solid guidance throughout each stage will keep your strategy on track. The Entrepreneur's Handbook provides that expert guidance. Over all ten stages of launching a startup, the guide will help you to translate your vision and ideas into concrete business plans by securing valuable relationships with vendors, investors, and potential customers.

CHAPTER 2

Finding Your Passion

Skills: The culmination of your passion and values leads to your skills. Deputy ran a comprehensive survey to learn more about the top 3 career goals for today's workforce. If you do these things, you'll increase your skills and reputation – that's true passion!

Value: Figure out what you are good at and align your goals with your expertise. After identifying your goals, ask yourself, "Do these objectives allow you to use your unique skills and abilities?" If not, refine your objectives and get to know your talents, achieve your career goals, and pick a company that exemplifies those core values. Learn more about yourself and discover the roles that suit your unique skills and strengths with Clifton Strengths.

Passion: This should be the easiest part - love what you do and do what you love. Your goals should reflect the things that you are passionate about. Creating prediction markets and polling? Share your enthusiasm by making it a family activity and collectively predict which movies will win the category for best picture during the Oscars.

You've probably heard this many times before, but it's because it's one of the most important steps of entrepreneurship. If you do not believe in yourself and what you are doing, no one else will believe in you either. People with passion can change the world. Before you know what your business or company should be doing, before you define your mission and vision, you must know what you stand for. You discover your core values by looking at three other components.

CHAPTER 3

Identifying a Market Opportunity

However, for startups, finding the right 'market opportunity' is particularly challenging. The challenge lies in the startup's limited team, experience, and access to potential customers or users. Lean startup method suggests quickly building a prototype to gather feedback and reiteration until the startup spots the killing customer scenario. However, in technology startups, the issue runs deeper - path-breaking ideas often do have few early customers or partners who understand the leap of technology and hence take the risk of becoming early customers or partners. In spite of the risk of failure, entrepreneurs do need to spot and commit to a market opportunity at a high level before they commit substantial resources and build a team to execute the idea. What is the solution? Entrepreneurship is not a science, and hence there isn't a set formula to follow, but we have put together seven practical steps that successful technology startups commonly followed to find their market opportunity.

Identifying a market opportunity: Entrepreneurs often have a general idea, but they are really seeking to develop a new disruptive or path-breaking technology-based product or service. This is something that creates a new industry segment or can ramp up the growth of an incumbent by adding a disruptive value proposition to the existing technology landscape. One of the key success criteria for any technology innovation is finding its value and demand in the already existing technology landscape. Insightful identification of the 'market opportunity' is as important as the brilliant technology or idea. In fact, successful technology projects are known for their successful design and are rarely recognized for their technology - IBM PC or Apple's iPhone are classic examples. In both cases, technology was known and existed, but it was these brilliant designs and value propositions that accelerated their adoption.

CHAPTER 4

Conducting Market Research

This is where market research helps us in a big way. By providing us a wealth of information supporting critical business decisions through learning business fundamentals, identifying problems, validating market strategies, planning strategy, and obtaining unbiased opinions. At the heart of market research, the desire to collect, collate and analyze data on market performance and customer attributes is probably why the internet is teeming with high quality free and paid resources such as for revenue projections and sales leads. While the above resources can be invaluable to a business, they could also deter many small business startups due to the fairly steep learning curve and the costs concerned.

As the excitement of turning a startup from an idea to reality (hopefully) begins to fade and the actuality of building, launching, and operating a business sets in, we quickly realize that the steep climb is far from over. The next important aspect in laying down the foundation of a business is conducting thorough market research. The goal of market research is to help you understand what your customers want, what they're willing to pay for it, and what you need to do to be successful. As we have learned from other startups, we cannot be in a position to build a lasting business merely by following our passion.

CHAPTER 5

Developing a Business Plan

To begin, it is important to understand the reason why your startup needs a plan. Formal business planning doesn't have to be a daunting process, but the importance of a plan that lays the direction for your company, communicates value to potential investors and other stakeholders, as well as the necessary steps for pursuing market growth, cannot be overstated. A business plan is considered a living document that can be modified at any time once the venture's operation is almost in place - even before it is profitable. Your business plan is a way to ensure that your company can become profitable as quickly as possible, or start to host the largest party in history for future mergers and acquisitions. A pragmatic plan ensures that your goals can be effectively delivered by responsible entities with specific budgets and deadlines. With those elements in place your team can monitor and improve toward the successful conclusion of the startup journey. You wouldn't travel to a new place without a map, so why would you want to start-up your company without a roadmap?

It's not enough to have a great idea - you need to think through the nuts and bolts, too. If you want to attract outside funding, your company's value proposition must also be clear (and that doesn't mean just promising to make money). Your business plan will articulate the vision for your startup by describing exactly what the company will be, do, and how you will achieve success. Guidance on aligning key elements of your business plan – including product and service descriptions, market research, target customer demographics, company organizational structure and business model - will be described. Sample business plan templates and outlines are provided for you as a guide.

CHAPTER 6

Securing Funding

Before you start talking to investors, you need to know your stuff. You should prepare a financial model of your company - a single-page pitch sheet. You should have believable revenue projections and expense projections over the next 12-24 months. It doesn't need to show a profit (in fact, it probably shouldn't), but it should show how you intend to make money and what you intend to spend it on. It should show some level of financial savvy. Additionally, it's not enough to just have a good idea and a good team executing on it to get money. You also need to show some sort of traction in the market. For consumer internet companies, this could be user growth, retention, and engagement. It could be product-market fit through customer interviews for B2B. And the most compelling traction is revenue. Money talks, and the more money you have, the more easily you'll be able to raise more. This goes for both young companies that need money and more mature companies that can't land big, game-changing deals. Make sure you can identify what your compelling traction is and show it in the pitch.

Funding is the lifeblood of any company. Most companies need outside investment for their initial startup, and many more need top-up money as time goes on. Funding can come from a variety of sources, ranging from professional venture capitalists to angel investors, to friends and family, to crowd-sourcing sites like Kickstarter. Each type of investor has its advantages and disadvantages, and different types and stages of funding are appropriate for different businesses.

CHAPTER 7

Building a Team

To help you better manage your networking, score it. In a different time from yours now, I read "Never Eat Alone" written by Keith Ferrazzi. He wrote about the tremendous importance of your networking capabilities (and not only those). I did not like the book too much because what was important was to spread the idea, so nothing further was irrelevant. But one thing caught my attention: the importance of tracking your networking effort. I made myself a method about that. I gave scores to people. One of these scores was just to understand how interested people were. Simple as that. Being seen looking at the telephone? 0.5. Having an interesting conversation? 7. This score helped me direct my networking focus to where the return would be much greater. After all, it is not because a person is successful today that their support will help you. Remember that success comes from performance and performance comes from success. And the "visitor" ("opportunist" in Brazilian corporate slang) had become a risk to navigate. A recognized risk. His idea score survived this selection. It is important to remember that it had already passed the credibility and personal values check.

As the idea for a business venture moves into reality, the need for a team is crucial. That doesn't mean you have to hire a team because it takes time to validate an idea, manage the early product development, and increase user adoption. You will most likely need validation on a specialized subject at a higher level than what your initial research was. You might need an advisor in your commercial area or tech if you are a business person or a tech one. The best way to get those who can help you is to network, network, and network.

CHAPTER 8

Creating a Product or Service

And that engine is your network. Network? Yes. Network. The idea that wins in the end is not the first person that came up with a product or the person who has the best widget. The idea that wins is the one with the most resilience and flexibility, that can adapt and grow in response to the myriad forces that will come to bear on it. You're never going to have a better view than once you've realized you're not the operator of the machine, but rather the subject of it, at least as an entrepreneur. You understand that building a product or service or company takes an act of congress, and that there are so many moving pieces, so many interconnected systems and so many mysterious forces united against you, that only with a great following can you possibly try and overwhelm them. But then on the other hand, once you've obtained that understanding and the following, you will stop fearing things that you shouldn't. You will banish ignorance, and fear with it, for the most part, will follow it. You will be at peace.

There are many misconceptions about what "creating a product" actually involves. Some entrepreneurs believe that the creative process is much like this painting analogy, and that ideas just come to them. As a result, they take an unrealistic approach to thinking they would be able to launch something that really stands out simply because they had the right idea. This is not the case. A great idea simply gives you a head start. It offers an opportunity, but it doesn't take you to the finish line. Your idea is like the wheels on a car. Granted, you can roll with an idea that's bad, but great wheels won't move you without a good engine.

Marketing and Sales Strategies

The options for getting customers are numerous, but the key is to use a cost-effective channel to reach potential customers. Startups must pick up customers one by one to create a large customer base, often through one-on-one relationships. Strong candidates typically include friends and family, who understand your solution and believe in you. But in order to test whether or not the solution is actually solving a problem or if it is just a "nice to have" requires a potentially much larger customer base. Various channel strategies must be tested and measured to determine what works best. No need to run expensive display ad campaigns or develop a mobile app that runs a heavy push notification campaign. Instead, blogs, user groups, meetups or maybe going out to the local dog park with some organic dog food samples in your pocket would be a better starting strategy. It is best to be very careful to avoid being overeager to spend money too soon.

Once you have selected a niche market, you need to figure out how you will connect with your target customer. In other words, you need to design a sales and marketing strategy. Everyone has different sales and marketing goals. However, your sales and marketing objectives should not be to make X amount of dollars, but rather to acquire Y amount of customers. This is because future revenues depend on customer acquisition and retention, both of which should be consistently managed through the marketing and sales efforts. As discussed in the sections above, focus on acquiring customers by offering value to them, not by taking shortcuts. Avoid black hat techniques that might make money in the short run, but will hurt businesses in the long term.

CHAPTER 10

Launching and Scaling Your Startup

Don't mistake me for someone with a better playbook. I'm still learning how Brand Creators will engage early adopters. I'm still learning what we can throw at scaling our low-cost, high-margin, fast-marketing draws new users every week, but also continues to bring people back. From the outset, we decided we wanted tiny, but predictable, flips or dumps, and always reinvested flips into the business. When necessary, we nixed sales to avoid blowing up customer expectations. Equally important, we never one-offed our product to save or create a flailing unit. We instead dug through every offer and made sure our average order size was increasing.

With so many moving parts, you need a guide to take your startup from idea to successful launch. Boiled down to three sheets, here's the last of a 10-part entrepreneurship-inspiring call-to-action: the Entrepreneurs Handbook that covers everything in a novel way - the five execution and five growth steps.

You'll also want these handy, so you can continue to fill in the answers as the big questions come up.